Copyright © 2023

All rights reserved. This book or any portion thereof may not be reproduced or used in any manner whatsoever without the express written permission of the author except for the use of brief quotations in a book review.

Printed in Australia

First Printing, 2023

ISBN 978-0-6453760-1-2

White Light Publishing

Warnbro, WA, 6169

whitelightuniversal.com

Dedication

I dedicate this book to my amazing husband, Peter, thank you for all your unconditional love and support. You always believe in me, and just be the most amazing husband!

To my 3 incredible children, Bianca, Sam and Roxanne, I'm so blessed to have you.

To my guides and loved ones in heaven, thank you for channelling these beautiful messages to me. My connection with spirit is a blessing that I'm lucky enough to be able to share. Bringing guidance, love, comfort and healing for others.

The messages in this book are channeled
messages from loved ones in heaven.

Michelle has been guided to write this
book for those times when you feel
lonely, need guidance, or just need
a loving message.

A daily message from Heaven

This beautiful little book holds within it channelled messages of love and guidance from your loved ones in heaven.

Every morning hold the book on your heart, think loving happy thoughts about your loved one. Feel them standing right next to you!

Gently allow the pages of the book to fall open, revealing a loving message for you from heaven. Allow yourself to be guided to open up to three pages, to bring in a short conversation with your loved one. Allow yourself to think over or even meditate on the message you receive.

Some days the message maybe from your loved one about what you need to know or do. Other times it may be a beautiful message from them about them.

Use this book every day or when you need a loving connection for reassurance and guidance.

The more you use this beautiful book, the deeper and stronger your ability to receive a very detailed message will develop. This will help you to develop your mediumship abilities. The book is black and white to allow your conscious mind to fill in the finer details. Your subconscious, intuition, will open and receive the rest of your message.

Pathway of the Soul

Leaving our earthly body and returning to spirit is as natural as the sun rising and setting, as the stars twinkling in the sky.

At the time of passing back to the spirit world our loved ones stay close to the earth plane until the time of the funeral and wake. This is when we say goodbye to them. They too are saying goodbye to the lifetime as who they were and the role they had. A new chapter of their journey is just beginning. A new chapter for you has also begun. You're now learning to live a life without them with you in the physical body.

How they passed, the age and time they were when they passed away is all part of a contract they agreed too, before they were born. Once a soul has returned to heaven / spirit they no longer have a gender, as a soul is both male and female. A soul, your soul is in fact gender neutral. It is one reason why a soul so desperately wants to experience a physical body. To have a sexuality, to have a gender. To experience touch, taste, smell, sex, emotions. To learn to love and become authentic with being true to themselves. Your soul, every soul has a personality, that is the result of numerous experiences both in heaven and on earth.

Each lifetime is a fractal particle of your soul, every soul. Every soul is learning to become an authentic fractal of consciousness. Macrocosm and Microcosm. As above, so below. This is something which needs much more detail, than can be briefly mentioned here.

Two guides, were appointed to watch over the lifetime. These guides are appointed by an angelic council. As the guides have experienced all that the lifetime to be lived is concerned with achieving. The two guides are with the soul at the time the contract is drawn and put in place. A soul becomes a guide once they no longer need to reincarnate. They have finished the wheel of incarnation into an earthly physical body. They have started a new journey of soul growth into the higher realms of the spiritual path. Guides are angels with L Plates. They have progressed through the lower realms of heaven and its learnings, to the first part of the journey into the angelic realms. Eventually all souls will progress to this point and then higher. Until complete union becomes possible, back with Source, or Consciousness, whatever term you feel comfortable to call the Creator.

Throughout your life there may be numerous different Spirit Teachers that enter your life to teach you new chapters. These Spirit Teachers specialise in the chapter you need to learn, as part of your earthly schooling, as a soul. When a new spirit teacher enters you will possibly find a new hobby, new interest, study a new course, begin a new way to live. The list is endless of possibilities which could open up. Your spirit teacher does your grading on the tests you encounter, as a result of your learning. Spirit Teachers are highly evolved souls, who have an extremely important role in many of the different stages of progression back to Divine Consciousness / Source / God.

Loved ones do not become your guide after passing. They do not have this contract with you! They have their own path to continue to follow after passing.

The first 3 months after someone has passed away, they spend healing, reflecting and reviewing the lessons, experiences, soul growth, achievements and consequences of the life they lived. The ego falls away. They no longer have any desire for the material concerns, objects, angers, achievements, belongings etc.

Your loved one will always be with you, as you have an unconditional bond that ties you together for eternity. They are with you in a moments thought.

Over time, the connection to the earth plane becomes weaker and weaker. The way of communication changes, to become telepathy. As all thoughts are the way of communication in heaven. There is no language. There is only energy that a soul is a part of. Part of all oneness. The longer they are in the place of oneness and all knowing the less and less they visit the earth plane.

As they are now moving forward with what their soul has planned for their own spiritual growth.

It is us here, who hold on to the person we loved. It is us who hold on to this earthly image of our loved one. They have finished this life. They have finished learning the lessons as who they were and what role they played. They are now moving forward to the next stage of spiritual growth.

This may be hard to fathom, as you so desperately want to hold them close, as who they were.

They are now in an all knowing energy where all thoughts are known.

The longer they are in this place the less and less they visit.

It's a natural process, it's unavoidable.

Remember you have probably had many lifetimes with your loved one and you'll probably have many more. The love bond you share is eternal! This allows you to always have them close by you. Until then you have this book to help you connect and receive messages of love from heaven.

Praise for With Love from Heaven

I absolutely love this book! It's given
me the connection I've been needing. X
Sharon

This book has allowed me to feel my mum.
Now I know she's still with me. Thank you ox
Donna

WOW! I feel a definite connection to my Dad
when I read my message every morning.
It's as if he's right in front of me! ❤
Mandy

Michelle I can't thank you enough!
When I open the book to read my message,
it's almost as if I can feel my husband's hand
on mine, helping open to the page!
Katherine

I am right here,
I have never left you.

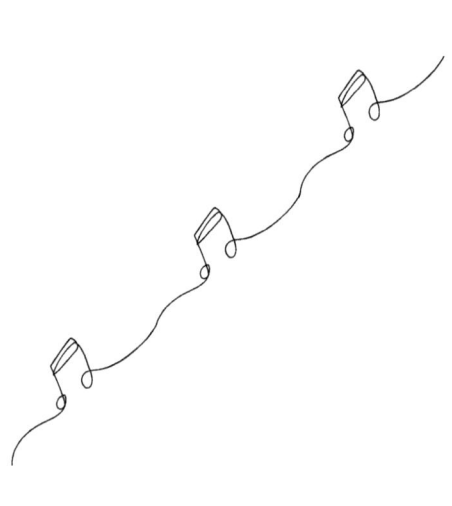

Everything happens for a reason.

*I can see you are hesitant.
Don't worry,
I will be helping you.*

Please stop beating yourself up. Everything will be ok.

I'm helping you hold your boundaries right now.

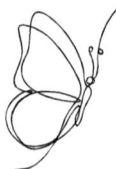

*I will always love you,
now, forever and always.*

*My passing was pain free.
I am free and happy.*

It was my time.

I'm watching over you right now.

Everything is going to be ok.

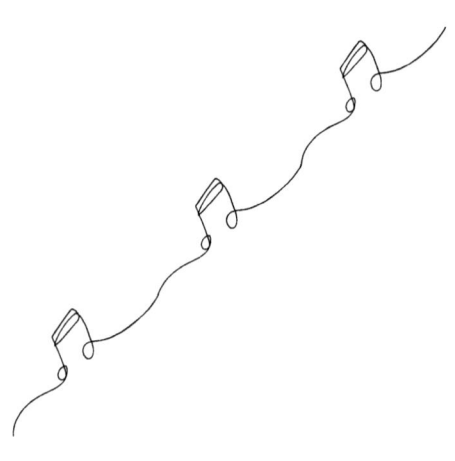

Don't beat yourself up any more.

I am with family.

You have so much to look forward to.

I will be here waiting for you.

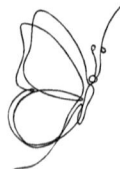

I watch over you every night.

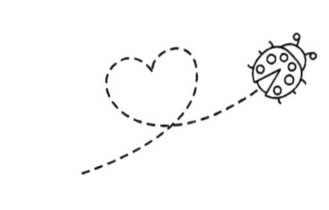

I visit you in your dreams.

Please don't be sad.

*I'm helping you,
one day at a time.*

Today is the perfect day to just be.

What's done is done.
Let it go.

Be kind to yourself
I hear your thoughts.

I believe in you right now.

It's never to late.

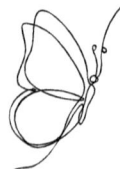

There is no time here.

Amazing new things are starting to happen for you.

We are connected by love.

Let go of your worries.

I now see everything so differently.

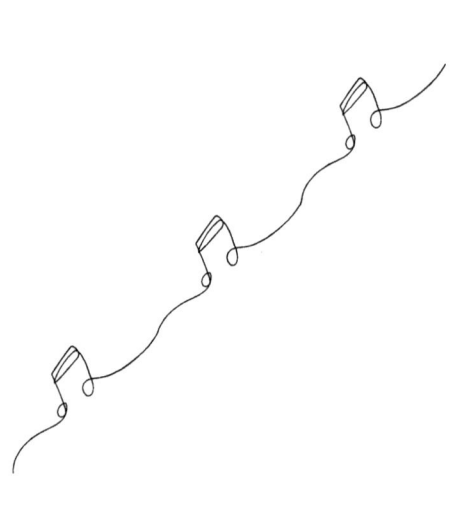

*It's very peaceful
and loving here.*

*I wish I had told you
I love you more.*

*Life is too short,
enjoy today.*

Remember to laugh.

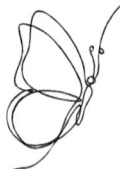

I am pain free now.

Thank you for the beautiful memories.

I had a good life.

I no longer have any concerns or worries about material objects.

My beautiful pets are with me.

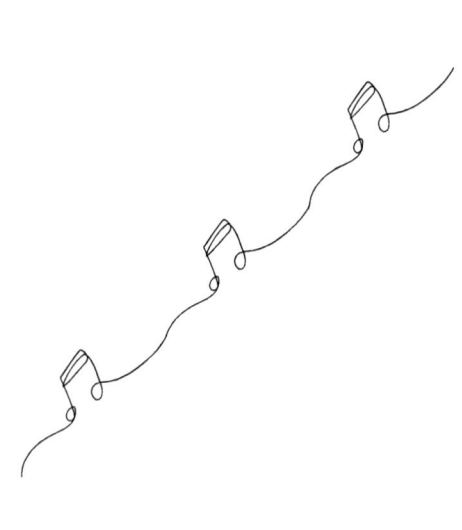

I'm helping you make the right decision.

*I had to leave
the way I did.*

It's not your fault.

*Thank you for
all your love.*

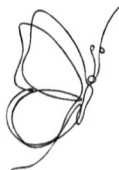

Life will soon get easier for you.

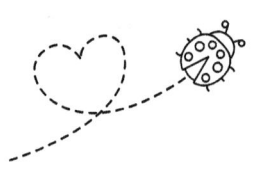

I hear everything you think about.

It's ok to move on.

You have many happy times yet to come.

I will be right there with you!

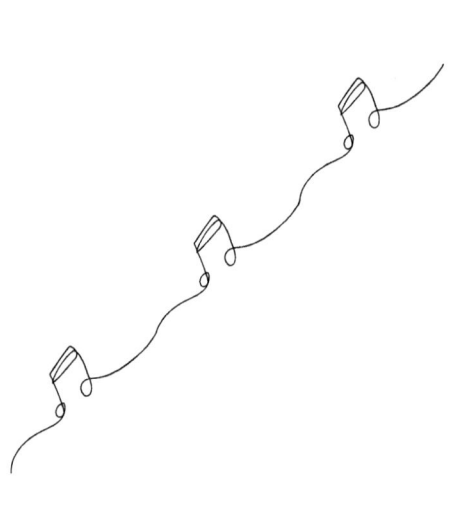

*When you suddenly
think of me.
I'm there with you!*

I'm always sending you signs.

Don't sweat the small stuff.

I no longer hold any grudges.

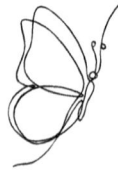

Please forgive me.

If I could I would live differently now.

*You always meant
the world to me.*

It doesn't matter in the bigger picture.

Don't waste time being upset with others.

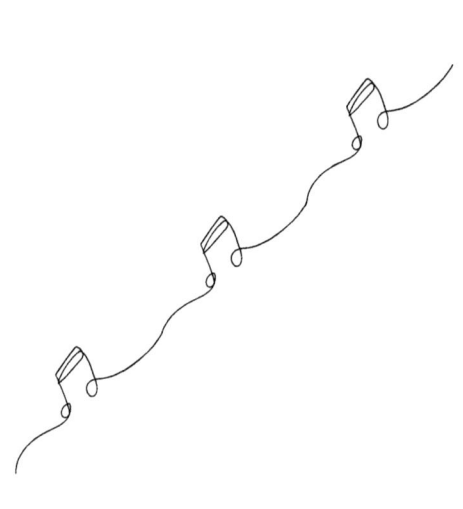

I forgive.

I have fully healed.

Good news is coming for you.

You can do it!

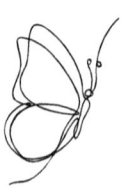

Yes!
It's going to be all right.

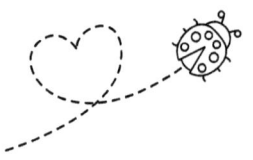

There was nothing you could have done.

*That's the way
it had to be.*

Each life time is a spiritual lesson.

We choose to have a physical life to learn.

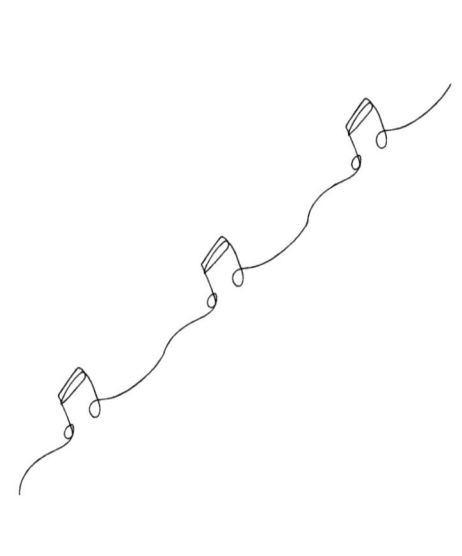

We are all connected by our thoughts.

What you think does matter.

It's time to step back.

Let go.

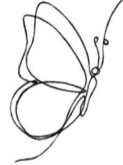

Remember to eat healthy.

*I'm showing you
the right way.*

Don't make the same mistakes.

Feel the answer within.

You know in your heart.

It's ok to take time for yourself.

It's so beautiful here.

*When you cry,
I cry too.*

*When you laugh,
I laugh too.*

*When I see memories
roll down your cheek,
I catch them with love.*

I give you a kiss good night.

Every morning I'm right there as you wake.

Relax I've got you.

I'll carry you those days you can't cope.

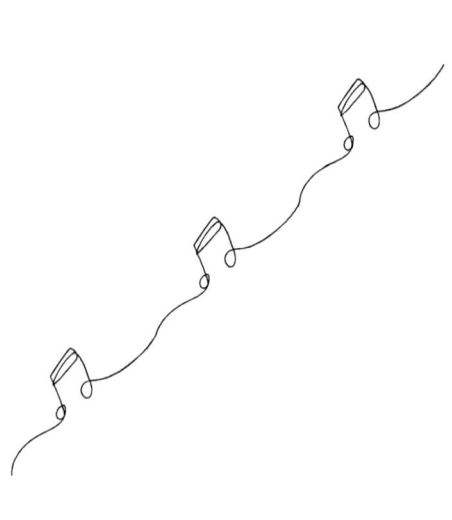

I'll be here for you.

There was no choice,
I had to go that way.

Everyone and Everything is connected.

*With love for
you always.*

You are very supported, right now and every day.

Never forget what it's taken you to get here.

*When you cry,
I'm right there, with you,
cuddling you.*

We will be connected forever with our love.

We are from the same soul family.

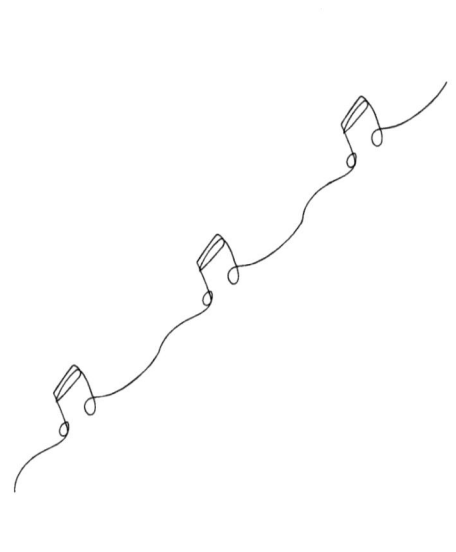

I was greeted by loving family.

There is so much more to understand, than you can comprehend right now.

*There are many different realms of souls,
I'm in heaven.*

*Don't give up,
this time will pass.*

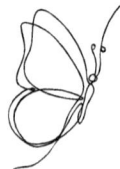

You have many loving family members and friends supporting you from heaven.

The colours here are amazing! There's more than you could ever imagine.

My loving arms are supporting you today and always.

Today I'm spending it with you.

*Be happy for me.
I am ok.*

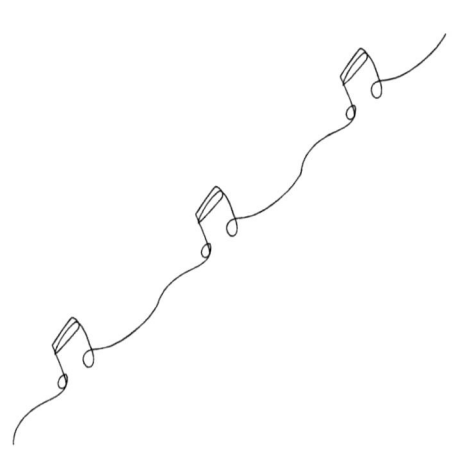

I wish I had known how to love you better.

Now I understand what my actions caused you.

I wish I had known how you felt before.

You can't always know.

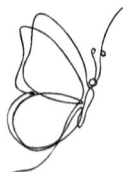

There is a reason for everything.

I'm asking you to forgive me, please, I'm so sorry I hurt you.

That was part of our learning together.

Karma can take many life times.

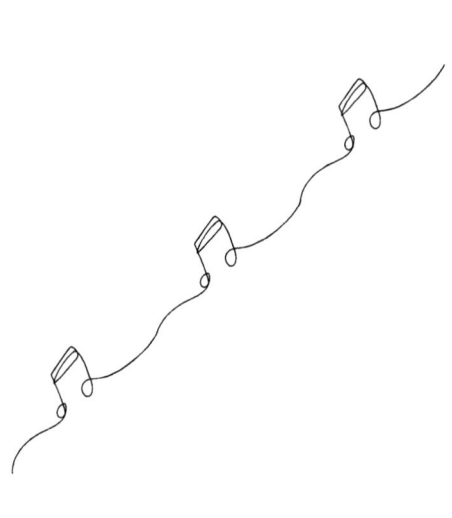

We will be together again soon.

Love is the answer.

In heaven we also have learnings and study time.

Praise for Michelle

Psychic Michelle Conway last night you gave me the most joy that I have felt since our little family of three have 'lost' allllllllllll of our closest loved ones including all four fur kids. We have been depressed, sad, angry, not getting along with each other...there is no love, happiness or wellbeing in our family or home. Last night you connected with my dear friend Russ...with smiles on your face, kindness, humour, I could sense with validation that he/they all are still right here even though we can't see, hear or feel them. You, Michelle, are a beautiful earth angel and I am so glad to have met you, am so glad Spirit led me to you last night!

Thank you sooooooooo much. I'm not quite sure how to get back the love, happiness and wellbeing in my family and home but for a couple moments last night...and some more waves (I've rewatched the video and reread my notes) when I remember our visit with Russ, it feels good...it feels like hope... I love and appreciate you, Michelle.
Love and hugs, me xo
Julie

I really enjoy being a part of those audience scenarios, I love to hear how you speak to people with real honesty and kindness, you are just so wonderful at what you do, and to see how people respond when they get a message from a loved one is just brilliant.
Thanks again, kindly,
Aisling

Hi Michelle, sorry I missed you today. Just wanted to thank you for being there for me through one of the most hardest stages of my life. I know that you would of felt alot was going on with me when you channelled in a drew card's for me. In August this year my partner took his own life. This year has been devastating for me but with your love and kindness of your spiritual gift you have helped me get up each day. I have still got a way to go but it's one day at a time. Anyways I just wanted to say thank you from the bottom of my heart. xx
Tash

Michelle Conway

Known as Australia's gentle psychic medium

Working within the arena of the psychic medium platform for almost 4 decades has given Michelle the privilege of reading for 1000's of people worldwide.

Spirit chose Michelle as a young child to be an ambassador for this work. As a result the journey has opened many different life experiences.

Working on an international psychic radio and T.V program, as well as regional radio stations in Victoria, has allowed Michelle to reach out to those who require genuine, honest, caring and accurate readings. Bringing from this answers, guidance, closure, healing and insight. Michelle works with spirit to bring all that is needed in the highest good for all.

Michelle has a Diploma in Counselling, Community Services, Grief & Loss, & Suicide Bereavement. Reikl Master, Diploma Bowen Technique, , Certificate 4 clinical massage, trained academic knowledge, as well as the window to knowledge from spirit, to assist all with healing, guidance, answers and closure. Which gives the assurance that you are in safe.

www.ingramcontent.com/pod-product-compliance
Lightning Source LLC
Chambersburg PA
CBHW050308010526
44107CB00055B/2155